God's Spies

and

Crossing the Bar

Two Short Plays

by Don Nigro

A Samuel French Acting Edition

SAMUELFRENCH.COM

God's Spies Copyright © 1983, 1985 by Don Nigro
Crossing the Bar Copyright © 1979, 1985 by Don Nigro

ALL RIGHTS RESERVED

Cover Image © Jose AS Reyes/Shutterstock

CAUTION: Professionals and amateurs are hereby warned that *GOD'S SPIES* and *CROSSING THE BAR* is subject to a Licensing Fee. It is fully protected under the copyright laws of the United States of America, the British Commonwealth, including Canada, and all other countries of the Copyright Union. All rights, including professional, amateur, motion picture, recitation, lecturing, public reading, radio broadcasting, television and the rights of translation into foreign languages are strictly reserved. In its present form the play is dedicated to the reading public only.

The amateur live stage performance rights to *GOD'S SPIES* and *CROSSING THE BAR* are controlled exclusively by Samuel French, Inc., and licensing arrangements and performance licenses must be secured well in advance of presentation. PLEASE NOTE that amateur Licensing Fees are set upon application in accordance with your producing circumstances. When applying for a licensing quotation and a performance license please give us the number of performances intended, dates of production, your seating capacity and admission fee. Licensing Fees are payable one week before the opening performance of the play to Samuel French, Inc., at 45 W. 25th Street, New York, NY 10010.

Licensing Fee of the required amount must be paid whether the play is presented for charity or gain and whether or not admission is charged.

Stock licensing fees quoted upon application to Samuel French, Inc.

For all other rights than those stipulated above, apply to: Samuel French, Inc., at 45 W. 25th Street, New York, NY 10010.

Particular emphasis is laid on the question of amateur or professional readings, permission and terms for which must be secured in writing from Samuel French, Inc.

Copying from this book in whole or in part is strictly forbidden by law, and the right of performance is not transferable.

Whenever the play is produced the following notice must appear on all programs, printing and advertising for the play: "Produced by special arrangement with Samuel French, Inc."

Due authorship credit must be given on all programs, printing and advertising for the play.

No one shall commit or authorize any act or omission by which the copyright of, or the right to copyright, this play may be impaired.
No one shall make any changes in this play for the purpose of production.
Publication of this play does not imply availability for performance. Both amateurs and professionals considering a production are strongly advised in their own interests to apply to Samuel French, Inc., for written permission before starting rehearsals, advertising, or booking a theatre.
No part of this book may be reproduced, stored in a retrieval system, or transmitted in any form, by any means, now known or yet to be invented, including mechanical, electronic, photocopying, recording, videotaping, or otherwise, without the prior written permission of the publisher.

ISBN 978-0-573-60168-2   Printed in U.S.A.   #9643

God's Spies

Originally commissioned by Actors Theatre of Louisville.

CHARACTERS

DALE — a woman of 25
WENDY — a girl of 19
CALVIN — a man of 22

SETTING

We are in a Christian Television station set, but all we see are three chairs in which Wendy, Dale and Calvin sit, Dale in the middle. Calvin is gangly and intense. Dale's hair looks like a wig but isn't. She is dressed up, with a little too much jewelry and makeup. Wendy is small and thin, no makeup, in a clean, faded Goodwill dress.

God's Spies

We are just about to go on the air. DALE is adjusting her skirt and checking her hairdo. WENDY is staring at her hands and squirming a bit. CALVIN crosses and uncrosses his legs.

DALE. (*to an invisible director down right*) What have we got, Jack, ten seconds? No? Don't be nervous, kids, God is on our side. At least, I hope he is. Is my hair all right? Feels like a bird nest. They got to stop using that spray gunk on it — it holds like elephant glue and smells like horse-sh — okay, here we go, smile, now — (*turning down front to the invisible camera, suddenly the genial hostess*) We're back. You're watching your Christian Youth Club on your Jesus Saves Network. I'm Dale Clabby and we're talking with Mr. Calvin Stringer about devil worship in modern music, and to Miss Wendy Trumpy, who spoke to God in a belfry.

WENDY. (*rather timidly*) Well, I didn't exactly —

DALE. (*turning from WENDY to CALVIN, not rudely but with a firm sense that she is in charge, and touching WENDY's hand briefly to reassure her*) Now, Calvin, you were telling us about this type of playing cards that are used in devil worship?

CALVIN. Yes, Dale, I've made a study of this problem and I don't want to alarm you ladies but what I discovered in my research is really shocking. I know *I* was shocked. Now, these here cards is called tarot cards — you pronounce it like it rhymes with carrot or parrot, or ferret — and you can find these cards all over the country, especially in the more subversive locations such as bookstores and universities. Now, these cards has got devil worshippin pictures all over em — one card is death with a big old weed-cutter in his hands, and one card is the devil hisself, and there's dogs and naked women with buckets and lobsters crawlin around—oh, Dale, I tell you, it ain't very nice at all, and your Satan worshippers will sling these here cards on the table and tell the future with em.

DALE. That IS shocking, Cal.

CALVIN. Oh, that ain't the half of it, Dale. I even discovered, in my research—and you're going to find this hard to believe, but it's true—I even found this one bookstore where you could buy these here Mickey Mouse tarot cards for little kids.

DALE. I don't believe that.

CALVIN. And they got these pictures of Mickey and Minnie Mouse and Donald Duck and Goofy, oh, it's horrible, Dale.

DALE. It sounds horrible.

CALVIN. Now, one of these here tarot card decks was made up by this man who is a self-confessed devil worshipper by the name of Aliston Crowley, this big bald-headed feller, and I tell you, Dale, this here Crowley deck is so obscene I could hardly even examine it.

DALE. Did you bring it with you?

CALVIN. I've got it at home, Dale. And if you look real close at this one album cover by this rock and roll group called the Blue Oyster Club, you can see real clear this Crowley feller standin right smack in the middle of a whole mess of them devil worshippers.

DALE. It's hard for me to accept that such a thing could be allowed to happen in a Christian nation like our own.

CALVIN. It's hard for me too, Dale, and it gets even more frightening when you trace this rock and roll music back to the Beatles in the sixties, and look at this one old Beatles album called Doctor Pepper's Lonely Hearts Cult Bands, you can see this big bald-headed feller with a six six six tattooed on his head.

DALE. Oh, no.

CALVIN. It's this Crowley feller again. Now it's my contention you can trace back the devil worship in this here Blue Oyster Club right back to Doctor Pepper through this Crowley feller back through these here ferret cards to the devil's worship and to Lucifer hisself.

DALE. Oh, dear.

CALVIN. That's true, Dale, and this Crowley feller he called himself the Great Beast of the Apocalypse, and he saw himself as the Antichrist, that's why he had the six six six on his head—and I believe that this man and these here Mickey Mouse ferret cards and these here Oyster albums is all a sign that the era of devil worship is upon us, that which is mentioned in the Revelations of Saint John the Divine which foreplays the ending of the world.

DALE. Oh, Calvin, that just makes me shudder all over my body.

CALVIN. Thank you, Dale, I feel the same way. And I'd also like to say a word or two about this group called Black Sabbath, and also about this one rock star feller who bites the heads off chickens and bats—

DALE. That's fine, Cal, thank you, we'll get back to you on that, but our director reminds me that we should turn now before our time is up on today's edition of the Christian Youth Club on your Jesus Saves Network to our second guest, Miss Wendy Trumpy, who talked to God in a belfry. Wendy, tell me, just how did you happen to come across God in a belfry? I mean, was this recently?

WENDY. No. I was a little girl.

DALE. Well, tell us about it, honey. Witness for the Lord. Don't be afraid.

WENDY. I'm not afraid.

DALE. Good.

WENDY. I was eatin breakfast.

DALE. In the belfry.

WENDY. In the kitchen. And I asked my mama where God was. And my mama said God was everywhere.

CALVIN. Praise Him.

DALE. Your mother was a wise woman.

WENDY. She was. She worked at the laundromat. And I asked my mama, I said, Mama, but where is God when he's at home? And my mama, who was trying to feed my baby brother Lumpy his Gerbers at the time, said, in heaven, sweetie. And so I asked her if we could go to heaven to visit him? And Mama said, no, honey, because you need an invitation to go to heaven, and ours ain't come right yet, but we can go to church and talk to God, because the church is God's house here on earth. And I said, okay, Mama, let's go see God today, because I got a few things I want to ask him, and Mama said, we can't today, honey, we got to feed Lumpy, but we'll go see him Sunday, okay? So I asked her if we could go to the zoo instead, and she said, Wendy, I think you better stay in the house today, because they said on the radio that a bad man had got out of the mental hospital and he wasn't very nice to little girls, and I'd better stay around close to home until they caught this man and put him away again, but I wanted to see God real bad, so I snuck out of the house while my mama was cleanin up where the cat had puked—I think it was just hairballs.

DALE. I see.

GOD'S SPIES

WENDY. And I went down Sycamore street because I remembered seein this old church down that way one time when we was drivin back from the Banks of the Wabash Festival and our own church was way across town, and I could see the steeple of this old church a ways down the block behind these old sycamore trees, and I remembered my mama sayin to me, this is the church, this is the steeple, open the doors and see all the people, and playin with my fingers, and I figured maybe this was the church she was talkin about, so I went up the steps and had a hard time gettin this real heavy old door open, but I did, and I went in, and it was all dark and cool in there, and there wasn't nobody around that I could see, but I could hear this little tap tap tapping sound, real tiny and hollow in that big empty church, and I followed the sound cause I thought it might be God hangin up pictures of Jesus or somethin, and I went down these twisted little steps at the back by the altar and down into the basement, and I come upon this real skinny old man.

DALE. But tell us about God and the belfry.

WENDY. I'm comin to that. This skinny old man was wearin this funny kind of dirty old shirt like the tops of my daddy's long johns, and he had on these old brown pants like Mr. Lucas at the garage, and he was in the corner in the basement tap tappin this little nail into this wooden box he was makin, looked like a coffin for a dog or a little kid or somethin, and he looked over and saw me, and he didn't say anything. And I asked him if he was God. And the old man looked at me a minute and he put down his hammer and took my hand, his hand was all brown and twisted up and yellow and smelled like my daddy's Camels—I mean, cigarettes, not real camels, my daddy had a cow but we sold it when we got cable tv, and this skinny old man took me to this little shelf he had, and he had these little wooden animals on it — there was a horse, and a pig, and a elephant, and a beaver — all kinds, and I asked him did he make all them animals, and he made this funny noise in his throat like he couldn't talk right, kinda like AAAAAA-AAAAAAA AAAAAAAAAAAAAAAAAAAA — (*Her demonstration is abrupt and rather loud and grotesque, startling DALE and CALVIN somewhat.*) — sorta like that, and then he showed me this funny kind of knife he had, and he was comin over towards me with this knife, I guess so I could see it better, and makin that AAAAAAAAAAAAAAA sound in his throat, when I heard the bells ringin upstairs, and he looked up, and I remembered that my mama would be lookin for me if I wasn't there for lunch, so I said goodbye and ran back up the stairs and there was this fat old pastor with a red face upstairs pullin on a rope to ring the bell, and I went over to the rope and looked up, and I could see all these steps curvin up the bell tower to where the bell was, and when this fat pastor saw me he stopped ringin the bell and said, What are you doin here, little girl? And I said, Talkin to God, but I got to get home now or my mama's gonna whup the shit outa me, and so I ran out and down the steps and all the way home and on the way I stubbed my toe on the crooked sidewalk and fell down and cut my knee, and I still got the scar here, see? (*She pulls up her dress to reveal the scar and most of her legs.*)

DALE. (*pulling WENDY's dress back down*) Well, that was certainly an inspiring story, Wendy. And I want to remind all the little children out there in Christian viewing land never to speak to strange old men with knives in basements, especially when they go AAAAAAAAAA.

CALVIN. You know, speakin of belfries, that reminds me about an interesting fact about this rock and roll feller who bites the heads off bats and chickens. See, this feller—

DALE. Calvin, I don't think—

WENDY. I ain't through yet. (*Pause. They both look at her.*)

DALE. Well, our time is almost up, Wendy, and—

WENDY. But I ain't through. I got to finish my witness.

DALE. Oh. Well, go on and finish, I didn't mean to interrupt. But try and condense it a bit, as we got to have some time at the end for Jack to tell the folks at home about our special Christian Youth Club Bible which only costs fifty-eight dollars this week only with a contribution and you get a free packet of Burpee melon seeds—

WENDY. You sell Bibles?

DALE. Well, these are very nice Bibles, they got gold around the edges of the pages and—

WENDY. Heck, don't them people know they can go to a motel and get a Bible for free?

DALE. But maybe our viewers can't afford to go to motels.

WENDY. Then how can they afford fifty-eight dollar Bibles?

DALE. Many of our viewers, Wendy, are shut-ins and bedridden, they can't get out to motels to get Bibles.

WENDY. There's folks'd give em Bibles. They don't have to pay no fifty-eight dollars for em. The Gideons'd give em Bibles. Ain't you never got one of them little green Bibles on the street? They're real nice folks, and they sure as hell don't charge no fifty-eight dollars for no Bibles.

DALE. But they don't give away Burpee seeds.

WENDY. Burpee seeds ain't worth no fifty-eight dollars. That's enough Burpee seeds to choke a goat.

CALVIN. Did the Blue Oysters send you to us, Wendy? I bet you got a six six six tattooed on some part of your body, don't you?

DALE. I think that's all we've got time for, now, so—

WENDY. I GOT TO FINISH MY WITNESS, NOW, YOU LET ME FINISH MY WITNESS, DON'T YOU CARE NOTHING ABOUT MY WITNESS? DO YOU PEOPLE CARE MORE ABOUT YOUR DAMN FIFTY-EIGHT DOLLARS THAN YOU DO ABOUT MY CHRISTIAN WITNESS? (*pause*)

DALE. No. Of course we don't. You go right ahead and give us your witness, dear. You just go right ahead. (*looking up towards the camera and past it*) No, it's all right, Jack, let's let her finish her witness. It's all right, go ahead, Wendy.

WENDY. Well, I went home, and my mama she whupped the livin bejesus out of me for leavin the house, and I tried to tell her I just went to the church to talk to God, and how he made these little wooden animals and coffins in the basement and made a noise like AAAAAAAAAAAA, but she thought I was lyin, and she said the bad old man what had done awful things to three little girls was still runnin loose, and she sent me to bed without supper and I was layin there in my room at night gettin awful hungry when I happened to think how hungry God must be down in that basement with nothin to eat—I could tell he didn't have nothin to eat because of how powerful skinny he was, and I remembered from the Methodist church that God liked to eat Welch's grape juice and little soda crackers, so I snuck out to the kitchen when they was all asleep and got me some grape juice and soda crackers and put em in a paper bag and went out through the yard real quiet and down the sidewalk in the dark towards the church, and I wasn't scared because I remembered I was bringin God somethin to eat so he wouldn't have to go out to Taco Bell or nothin while he was workin so hard on his animals, and the church door was unlocked, and I went inside and it was dark in there, too, but there was a candle or two burnin down by the altar, and I found my way to the steps and down into the basement but I couldn't find nobody down there in the dark so I went back upstairs and I started sayin real quiet, God? Here God. Here, sir, I brung you some crackers. I come to where the bell rope hung at the bottom of the belfry and I looked up them twisted stairs up to where the bell was and I thought maybe God had gone up there to look at the moon, so I took my paper bag all the way up them steps, and when I stopped to rest about half way up I thought I could hear somebody down the steps a ways walkin up behind me, but then it stopped, and when I looked back down the steps I couldn't see nothin but the shadows, so I kept goin up till I got to the top, but I couldn't find God up there neither, and I was real tired from the climb, so I went and sat on the sill of this little window up there, and it was open, and the air smelled real cool and nice, and there was a moon and I could see stars out and everything real tiny down below, it was awful high up, and I thought I heard somebody again, and I looked back towards the stairs and there was somebody comin up towards me, but I still couldn't see who it was, and he kept comin towards me, and I thought it must be God, and I said, Hi, God, I brung you some Welch's grape juice and soda crackers, and he started sayin what a pretty little girl I was, and how soft I looked, and how he liked my hair, and then I knew it wasn't God because I knew from the morning that God doesn't talk, or if he does talk it ain't so you can rightly understand him, cause it just sounds like AAAAAAAAAAAAAAA or something, and he stepped into the moonlight and I seen it was that fat old pastor from that mornin who'd asked me what I was doin there, only now he didn't look so nice, and he was sayin how he liked my little soft legs and how evil I was and he was comin at me and sayin these really awful things at me I didn't half know what they meant even but I didn't like the sound of em and his face was all red and sweaty and then he kind of made a grab at me and I sort of hung out the window a bit standin on the sill there and he come up real close and he smelled real bad and that fat pastor's face was so red I thought it was gonna explode like a big old rutabaga and then I knew I'd gone lookin for God and come to the wrong place and found the Devil by mistake, and I commenced to screamin, and then the devil he reached out his big old fat sweaty hands to touch me when the bell started ringin. The bell was right behind him you see and all of a sudden it jumped and clanged real loud, and the Devil he musta had bad nerves because when it rung all sudden like that he kinda turned half around towards it whilst still movin in my direction and he whacked his shins against the windowsill and flung his arms out and went flyin backwards out into the air like a big black cow in a crow-suit, and he plopped down on the sidewalk way down there and I looked down and I could see then it wasn't the Devil, it just looked like some old scarecrow somebody had threw away. And the bell had stopped ringin and it was real silent. And when the policemen came I told them all about it and they looked for God but they couldn't find him, and they never did figure out who rang the bell. (*pause*)

CALVIN. Well, what that teaches us, Wendy, is that the Devil is everyplace, and we got to be careful to watch where we step, because—

WENDY. No it don't. It don't teach us nothin of the sort. It teaches me that somebody like you that goes lookin for the Devil every damn place he goes is a damn idiot. I tell you, Dale, what I did find, though, I found this little wooden pony in the basement there, I got it right here in my purse, and I brought it here to give to you, Dale, because when my grandma was real sick and in bed she used to love to watch your show every day, and it gave her pleasure, and I just wanted you to have this, I kept it all this time, and it's for you, but it won't cost you no fifty-eight dollars, cause it's a present. (*She holds out the wooden animal towards DALE.*)

DALE. You want to give that to me?

WENDY. Yes mam.

DALE. But that must be important to you, I mean—

WENDY. Well, I expect it was important to God, but he give it to me, and now I'm givin it to you, on account of my grandma. (*She holds it out to DALE again.*)

CALVIN. You watch out there, Dale, don't you touch that, now, that's a instrument of the Devil, for the Lord says thou shalt not make no gravy images, and she come straight from them Blue Oyster people, I just know she did, and—

DALE. Oh, hang it up, Calvin. (*Pause. CALVIN looks at her, hurt. DALE takes the animal.*) Thank you. Thank you very much. (*She looks at the animal.*) It's really very nice.

WENDY. Dale, I think that man over there on the other side of the camera is tryin to get your attention.

DALE. Oh. Well, uh, yes, I guess that's all we have time for today, so, until next time, good luck, praise God, and remember to send in for one of our Christian

Youth Club Bibles, they got big print and color pictures of the Holy Land and—(*brief pause*)—and also, they're free. You just send in your name and address and we'll send you one for free.

WENDY. Dale, why is that Jack fella jumpin around and wavin his arms like that? Is he havin a conniption fit or somethin?

DALE. I don't know, honey, I expect he's just got the Holy Spirit in him. This is Dale Clabby, until next time, saying, God loves you, and I do the best I can. Amen.

(Blackout)

Crossing the Bar

CROSSING THE BAR was first presented on WISU Radio in Terre Haute, Indiana on January 28, 1979 with the following cast:

GRETCHEN .... Donna Harlan
MARGARET .... Su Causey
CORPSE.............................. Kim Hedges

The production was directed by Geoff Hammill.

CHARACTERS

MARGARET — an old lady
GRETCHEN — her friend
CORPSE — a dead person

SETTING

A funeral parlor. An open coffin. Flowers around. Folding chairs.

Crossing the Bar

A funeral parlor. In the background, very softly, an organ plays 'Nearer My God To Thee,' rather lugubriously. MARGARET and GRETCHEN sit on folding chairs before an open coffin. Flowers. Beside MARGARET's chair, an umbrella.

MARGARET. My, doesn't he look nice.
GRETCHEN. He's lovely.
MARGARET. It's a great tragedy.
GRETCHEN. He was a very nice man.
MARGARET. God wastes so much.
GRETCHEN. He works in mysterious ways, Margaret.
MARGARET. Enigmatic.
GRETCHEN. Labyrinthine.
MARGARET. Phantasmagoric.
GRETCHEN. A very great tragedy.
MARGARET. Like *King Kong*.
GRETCHEN. *King Lear*.
MARGARET. Yes.
GRETCHEN. He was a nice little boy, too. Always polite. Treated his Aunt Fanny with respect. Never poured salad oil down her ear trumpet like the other boys.
MARGARET. Vinegar.
GRETCHEN. Yes.
MARGARET. Loved those elderberry pies.
GRETCHEN. Loved those pies. He surely did.
MARGARET. He was popular with young people and old people alike, fat and thin, smart and stupid, rich and normal. Everybody.
GRETCHEN. The dead.
MARGARET. The unborn.
GRETCHEN. Fish.
MARGARET. Yes.

GRETCHEN. Everybody loved him.
MARGARET. I did.
GRETCHEN. And smart as a whip.
MARGARET. Snap.
GRETCHEN. He did love animals so.
MARGARET. And they loved him.
GRETCHEN. Oh, my, yes. They'd often follow him home.
MARGARET. I remember that.
GRETCHEN. You could look out the front window and see whole packs of wild dogs following him down the yellow line on the highway.
MARGARET. What a sight.
GRETCHEN. And the birds.
MARGARET. Shit everywhere.
GRETCHEN. When I think of the birds I have to smile.
MARGARET. I laugh.
GRETCHEN. I also laugh.
MARGARET. Ha ha.
GRETCHEN. Ha ha ha.
MARGARET. Shit everywhere.
GRETCHEN. Used to land on his shoulders and eat right out of his hands.
MARGARET. The birds.
GRETCHEN. Yes, the birds.
MARGARET. I thought so.
GRETCHEN. He was one of God's chosen.
MARGARET. Don't I know it.
GRETCHEN. He was one of the LOVELIEST—(*Her voice breaks and she stops.*)
MARGARET. Hang on, Gretchen. (*They are beginning to sniffle.*)
GRETCHEN. I can't help it. He looks so sweet.

MARGARET. He's a work of art. (*MARGARET blows her nose.*)
GRETCHEN. Wipe your nose.
MARGARET. I have sinus. It's going to rain.
GRETCHEN. No it's not.
MARGARET. I brought my umbrella.
GRETCHEN. Circumstantial evidence.
MARGARET. What are we going to do without him, Gretchen? Every Friday night he'd come calling. Every Sunday morning, off to church.
GRETCHEN. His saxophone.
MARGARET. Sunday afternoons, singing hymns around the old saxophone.
GRETCHEN. Those days will never come again.
MARGARET. 'Rock of Ages.' 'The Three Little Fishies.' 'The Battle Hymn of the Republic.'
GRETCHEN. That was my favorite. (*MARGARET blows her nose. GRETCHEN blows her nose a bit louder. MARGARET, a shade irritated, blows her nose louder still. Pause.*)
MARGARET. Don't you think he looks nice?
GRETCHEN. Gorgeous. Voluptuous.
MARGARET. As beautiful as in life.
GRETCHEN. Oh, better.
MARGARET. Do you think so?
GRETCHEN. Oh, yes, much better. They've put makeup over the carbuncle. See? (*She points.*)
MARGARET. Point discreetly, dear.
GRETCHEN. I always do.
MARGARET. I believe you're right, Gretchen. That was clever of them.
GRETCHEN. I think they did something to his nose, too.

MARGARET. His nose?
GRETCHEN. It isn't quite as peculiar looking as it was.
MARGARET. They DID, didn't they? My stars.
GRETCHEN. And garters.
MARGARET. Isn't it marvelous what they can do?
GRETCHEN. You can hardly tell it's the same nose.
MARGARET. Gretchen?
GRETCHEN. Yes?
MARGARET. You don't suppose they gave him someone else's nose.
GRETCHEN. Oh, I don't think so, dear.
MARGARET. I suppose you're right. He does look like himself.
GRETCHEN. He looks very much like himself.
MARGARET. In fact, when you think about it, it's really amazing how much he DOES look like himself, considering that he's dead and all.
GRETCHEN. It's a miracle. Praise God.
MARGARET. That man should get down on his knees and thank God he looks so much like himself. Amen.
GRETCHEN. Just look at the way his face is twitching like it always did.
MARGARET. Look at him twitch.
GRETCHEN. He looks exactly like himself when he twitches like that. (*pause*) Is he supposed to be twitching? Is that normal?
MARGARET. Good GOD, Gretchen, this man is twitching.
GRETCHEN. It's alive. Margaret, it's alive. Quick, rub his hands.
MARGARET. I don't want to touch his hands.
GRETCHEN. Rub all over his body.
MARGARET. Well. (*She considers.*) All right. What

the hell. (*They begin rubbing.*) Is he still twitching?

GRETCHEN. Try to sit him up. Come on. (*They try.*) Ooof. Urg. Watch out.

MARGARET. He's heavy.

GRETCHEN. Come on, Margaret, we can do it, get him sitting. Watch out. Get your hand off of there.

MARGARET. Off of where? (*The CORPSE is sitting up.*)

GRETCHEN. There. We've sat him. (*The CORPSE wobbles.*)

MARGARET. Look out. There he goes. (*The CORPSE falls back. Thud.*)

GRETCHEN. Oh, my God.

MARGARET. Fiddlesticks. Smashed his head a good one, too. Try to be more careful.

GRETCHEN. Get him again.

MARGARET. All right, all right. (*They try again.*) Urf. Ug. It won't stay up. It won't stay up.

GRETCHEN. Don't panic, Margaret.

MARGARET. (*trying to keep the CORPSE sitting*) Well I can't hold him up forever. Is he twitching?

GRETCHEN. Don't lose control.

MARGARET. I can't stand this. I'm hysterical. I'm hysterical.

GRETCHEN. Get the umbrella, quick.

MARGARET. Umbrella? The umbrella? What the hell do we need the umbrella for? Is it raining?

GRETCHEN. We'll prop him up with it.

MARGARET. Oh. Good thinking. (*She gets the umbrella.*) Here it is. How do we do this?

GRETCHEN. Wedge it there between the inside of the coffin and his back. There. Got it? (*The CORPSE is somewhat propped.*)

MARGARET. All right. (*The CORPSE begins to weave and slant.*) Woops. Upsy daisy. (*She rights him.*) There. All right.

GRETCHEN. Now let go. (*MARGARET does. Pause.*) It stopped twitching. Twitch. Come on. Twitch. (*She slaps his face a few times.*)

MARGARET. I think we've lost him, Gretch.

GRETCHEN. Nonsense. Sing.

MARGARET. Sing?

GRETCHEN. Loud. Right in his ear.

MARGARET. What should I sing?

GRETCHEN. I don't care. Anything.

MARGARET. All right. All right. Don't get testy. (*She bursts into song, the opening lines of "Indian Love Call."*)

GRETCHEN. (*slapping him*) WAKE UP. COME ON.

MARGARET. That's all I know.

GRETCHEN. Keep singing. Louder.

MARGARET.
BE KIND TO YOUR WEB FOOTED FRIENDS
FOR A DUCK MAY BE SOMEBODY'S UNCLE—

GRETCHEN. (*slapping him violently*) COME ON, SOLDIER. JUDGEMENT DAY. WAKE UP.

MARGARET.
BE KIND TO YOUR FRIENDS IN THE SWAMP
WHERE THE WEATHER IS VERY VERY GLUMP—

GRETCHEN. That's not the words.

MARGARET. Well I don't KNOW the words. What difference does it make?

GRETCHEN. Margaret, it's going to sneeze.

MARGARET. Who is?

GRETCHEN. Well who do you think?

CORPSE. (*sneezing violently*) AAAAAAAAAAAAA-AACCHHHHHHHHHOOOOOOOOOOO.

MARGARET & GRETCHEN. (*severally*) EEEEEEEKK-KKK. AAAAAHHHHHHHHHHH. OOOOOOO. EEEEEEK. (*pause*)

MARGARET. Gesundheit. (*The CORPSE collapses again with a great awful thud, the umbrella falls.*)

GRETCHEN. QUICK, GET HIM UP BEFORE HE CROAKS AGAIN. No, wait, artificial respiration.

MARGARET. I can't do that.

GRETCHEN. I'll do it.

MARGARET. I'll do it.

GRETCHEN. No, I'll do it.

MARGARET. I'll do it.

GRETCHEN. You touch that mouth and I'll shove this umbrella up your ear.

(*The CORPSE begins in a raspy, croaky voice to sing "Indian Love Call."*).

GRETCHEN & MARGARET. EEEEEEEEEEEEEK.

CORPSE. Betty?

GRETCHEN. No, dear, we're not Betty. We're Gretchen and Margaret. You remember Gretchen and Margaret. Elderberry pies. Forty years of sporadic and half-hearted courtship. Down the drain with yesterday's begonias.

CORPSE. Hurry up, Betty, I can't wait.

GRETCHEN. It's Gretchen. You remember Gretchen. Fried chicken. Boiled chicken. Baked chicken. Chicken on a stick.

MARGARET. Who the hell is Betty?

CORPSE. Nipples.

MARGARET. Betty Nipples?

CORPSE. Yes Betty yes Betty yes.

MARGARET. I used to make Brown Betties.

GRETCHEN. I don't think that's what he means.
CORPSE. Go Betty go Betty go.
MARGARET. This is rather shocking.
CORPSE. Call of the wild gull. Betty in the underbrush.
GRETCHEN. I don't like this. I don't like this at all. Who IS this Betty? Did she come to the funeral? Did SHE pick out the little invitations? Did she bring a cake?
CORPSE. Betty in the wildwood. Boom of the boomer squirrel. Rutting of beaver, Betty and me.
MARGARET. This man is spoiling a beautiful funeral.
CORPSE. Betty in the boondocks trembling. Betty in the night with purpley moonbeam, Betty in the back seat groaning, Betty of the magic fingers, Betty in the tall grass twisted moisty, Betty in the clutch, I'm coming, Betty, wait for me. (*The CORPSE tries to clamber out of the coffin.*)
MARGARET. Now wait just a minute. Get back in there. Betty isn't here. Gretchen, he's trying to get out.
GRETCHEN. I can see that.
CORPSE. Betty.
MARGARET. That's the rudest thing I've ever seen in my life. You just get right back in there, now. (*She is struggling with him. Fortunately for the women, he moves very slowly and awkwardly.*) Gretchen, help me.
CORPSE. Betty of the milk white breast.
MARGARET. Get back in that casket. GRETCHEN.
GRETCHEN. (*Roused, she takes action.*) Grab his head. The foot. Get the foot. (*a great awkward three way struggle*)
CORPSE. Urf. Ukk. Grkkk. Betty. Arlm.
GRETCHEN. Stop it. Stop that. Urf. Ek. You're DEAD, dammit, and that's all there is to it.

MARGARET. If you think—get his leg—urk—we've gone to all this trouble—uk—watch out—urf—for nothing—EEK—urk—the day lilies and the music and the beautiful memorial tombstone and the lovely plot overlooking East Liverpool—

CORPSE. Betty of the rubbery legs, Betty the woodland sylph, Betty the dream of the rood—BETTY— (*They manage to push him back down into the coffin, where he lands with a loud thud. Pause. The old women are breathing heavily.*)

GRETCHEN. Praise God.

MARGARET. What a struggle.

GRETCHEN. Is he moving?

MARGARET. I don't think so.

GRETCHEN. Watch him. The eyes are open.

MARGARET. No respectable dead person would act like that.

GRETCHEN. I wouldn't.

CORPSE. (*weak and pathetic*) Betty in the surf with your hair wet.

MARGARET. I never *did* like him. Always was a smart alec. Him and that stupid saxophone.

CORPSE. Betty in the shower squeaky.

GRETCHEN. Hogging down elderberry pies.

CORPSE. Betty on the rug with candles.

MARGARET. How many Betties has this man had?

GRETCHEN. It's disgusting.

MARGARET. Depraved. It's depraved.

CORPSE. Betty by the train wave bye bye.

GRETCHEN. God only knows what he was doing with all those dogs following him around.

CORPSE. Betty by the train wave bye bye.

MARGARET. Not to mention the birds.

GRETCHEN. That's too horrible even to think about.

CORPSE. Betty in the sea, the ocean green, the waves wash up, the jelly fish, the sand and the moon's eye, Betty in the sand by moonlight, Betty by the train wave bye bye.

MARGARET. MORPHODITE!

GRETCHEN. BIRD PERVERT!

MARGARET. I'LL BET THAT ISN'T YOUR REAL NOSE, YOU OLD HORNY!

CORPSE. Betty by the train wave bye bye.

GRETCHEN. Where's the umbrella?

MARGARET. Here.

CORPSE. Betty by the train wave bye bye.

GRETCHEN. (*thwacking the CORPSE violently over the head with the umbrella*) TAKE THAT. THAT. TAKE THAT. TAKE THAT. AND THAT. (*pause*) AND TAKE THAT. (*thwack*) AND ONE FOR BETTY. (*Thwack. Pause. The old women breathe heavily.*)

MARGARET. Is it moving?

GRETCHEN. I doubt it.

MARGARET. Are you sure?

GRETCHEN. Not a twitch. (*pause*)

MARGARET. God works in mysterious ways.

GRETCHEN. Yes. (*pause*) He certainly does. (*pause*)

MARGARET. See how peaceful he looks now?

GRETCHEN. Yes.

MARGARET. He's lovely. He looks just like himself. Doesn't he look like himself? He looks exactly—

GRETCHEN. Shut up, Margaret. (*In a burst of rage, GRETCHEN seizes the lid of the coffin, swings it up on its hinges and slams it shut. Pause.*)

MARGARET. He was such a wonderful man, though. It seems like such a waste. God works in mysterious ways. (*pause*) Gretchen, do you know anyone named Betty?

GRETCHEN. I don't want to talk about it.

(*Pause. Then, from inside the closed coffin, the CORPSE can be heard singing, quite beautifully, the closing words of "Indian Love Call," as the lights fade to darkness.*)

Also By
Don Nigro

Armitage

Martian Gothic

Nebuchadnezzar

Pandemonium

Punch and Judy

The Shadows

Tainted Justice

Traitors

The Winkleigh Murders

Please visit our website **samuelfrench.com** for complete descriptions and licensing information

OTHER TITLES AVAILABLE FROM SAMUEL FRENCH

ARMITAGE
Don Nigro

Mystery / 6m, 6f / Unit set

Zachary Pendragon rages among the tombstones of the family burial plot. Filled with hatred and waiting for him to die, his stepdaughter Margaret watches from their Gothic mansion in the east Ohio woods. So begins the dark and labyrinthine tale of a family with a complex and terrible history. Through Margaret's journal, Zach's memories, the batty poetry of Margaret's mother, and the memories of Zach's tormented son John, a Gothic tale woven back and forth in time and space emerges. It is a tale of desperate love and suspicious deaths, of desire, murder, madness, grief and terror. Having the richness and beauty of a complex Gothic novel or a Jacobean nightmare, this remarkable saga of happenings in the Pendragon mansion builds to a stunning conclusion that is guaranteed to surprise. Perhaps the most haunting of the author's cycle of Pendragon Plays, this mystery is both funny and grotesque, moving and hypnotic

SAMUELFRENCH.COM

OTHER TITLES AVAILABLE FROM SAMUEL FRENCH

MARTIAN GOTHIC
Don Nigro

2m, 3f / Unit Set

Commissioned by The Ensemble Studio Theatre in New York as part of the Alfred P. Sloan Foundation Science & Technology Project and developed earlier at the McCarter Theatre in Princeton, this controversial play traces the emotional conflicts of Sonia Pretorius, beautiful, brilliant and articulate spokesperson for the nuclear power industry, and her conflicts with her scientist father, her green sister, her frazzled and lovesick boss and her father's cynical girlfriend. As Sonia's world begins to collapse around her, the tension in her grows and moves her closer and closer to a meltdown.

SAMUELFRENCH.COM

www.ingramcontent.com/pod-product-compliance
Lightning Source LLC
Chambersburg PA
CBHW072023290426
44109CB00018B/2323